In Session

Jeff Beck

International Music Publications Limited
Griffin House, 161 Hammersmith Road, London W6 8BS

**DON'T BE
A MUSIC
COPYCAT!**

The copying of © copyright
material is a criminal offence
and may lead to prosecution.

Series Editor: Sadie Cook

Music Transcription, Arrangement and Recording: Martin Shellard
Music Editorial & Project Management: Artemis Music Limited
Cover Photo:
All photos supplied by Redferns Music Picture Library
Design & Production: Space DPS Limited
Reproduced and printed by Halstan & Co. Ltd., Amersham, Bucks., England

Published 1999

© International Music Publications Limited
Griffin House, 161 Hammersmith Road, London W6 8BS

Exclusive Distributors:

International Music Publications Limited

England: Griffin House
161 Hammersmith Road
London W6 8BS

Germany: Marstallstr. 8
D-80539 München

Denmark: Danmusik
Vognmagergade 7
DK1120 Copenhagen K

Italy: Via Campania 12
20098 San Giuliano Milanese
Milano

Spain: Magallanes 25
28015 Madrid

France: 20 Rue de la Ville-l'Eveque
75008 Paris

WARNER BROS. PUBLICATIONS U.S. INC.

USA: 15800 N.W. 48th Avenue
Miami, Florida 33014

Australia: 3 Talavera Road
North Ryde
New South Wales 2113

Scandinavia: P.O. Box 533
Vendevagen 85 B
S-182 15 Danderyd
Sweden

InSession with

Jeff Beck

In the Book...

On The CD...

Track 1	Tuning Tones	
Savoy		
Track 2	Full version	
Track 3	Backing track	
Track 4	Solo Section (full version) slow speed	
Track 5	Solo Section (backing track) slow speed	
Starcycle		
Track 6	Full version	
Track 7	Backing track	
Track 8	Solo Section (full version) slow speed	
Track 9	Solo Section (backing track) slow speed	
Big Block		
Track 10	Full version	
Track 11	Backing track	
Track 12	Solo Section (full version) slow speed	
Track 13	Solo Section (backing track) slow speed	
Led Boots		
Track 14	Full version	
Track 15	Backing track	
Track 16	Solo Section (full version) slow speed	
Track 17	Solo Section (backing track) slow speed	
Jeff's Boogie		
Track 18	Full version	
Track 19	Backing track	
Track 20	Solo Section (full version) slow speed	
Track 21	Solo Section (backing track) slow speed	
El Becko		
Track 22	Full version	
Track 23	Backing track	
Track 24	Solo Section (full version) slow speed	
Track 25	Solo Section (backing track) slow speed	

Biography

For as long as there has been rock guitar, one man above all others has been at its cutting edge, and that man is Jeff Beck. From his early days with The Yardbirds, when he helped pioneer the use of distortion and feedback, through to his jazz-rock collaborations in the 70s, to his latest incarnation as the godfather of rock guitar, Beck's playing has always been innovative and exciting.

Born on June 22nd 1944 in Wallington, Surrey, Jeff showed an interest in music from an early age, trying his hand at piano, violin and cello as well as singing in the school choir. He studied, for a while, at Wimbledon Art College but it was seeing Buddy Holly and Gene Vincent in concert and listening to his sister's American rock 'n' roll records that inspired him to play guitar.

He played in a couple of bands between 1961 and 1963 including The Deltones – a covers band that played Eddie Cochran and Shadows material.

In 1964 he left college and began to make his living as a guitarist. He made a name for himself as a rock 'n' roll guitarist and, whenever a hot guitar break was called for it was usually Beck that got the call. Around this time he met and became friendly with Jimmy Page, and when Page was asked to replace Eric Clapton in The Yardbirds, he recommended Jeff Beck. The Yardbirds were one of the first bands to translate high-energy blues into rock music and Beck's fiery style fitted them perfectly.

Beck's first recordings with The Yardbirds were on the FOR YOUR LOVE album but it was the 1965 hit *Heart Full Of Soul* from the album HAVING A RAVE UP that brought his first real acclaim. This is one of the first pop songs to feature Eastern-influenced guitar and also one of the first recorded uses of a fuzz-box. The story goes that the band hired an Indian sitarist to play on the single but he had trouble playing in Western 4/4 time. Beck, being a natural mimic, copied the sitar part on guitar and that's what you hear on the record.

During his time in The Yardbirds Jeff Beck became a flamboyant character and showman – on stage he would use distortion and feedback, playing with the guitar behind his head or back. The combination of massive volume and a reckless approach was captivating audiences everywhere, including a certain promising guitarist by the name of Jimi Hendrix, who later used these same techniques himself.

On THE YARDBIRDS album Beck recorded an instrumental showcase called *Jeff's Boogie* that highlighted not only his guitar prowess but also his love for fifties rock 'n' roll. The track is based on a Chuck Berry tune and is heavily influenced by Les Paul and the Gene Vincent sideman Cliff Gallup. Beck has often mentioned Gallup as a major influence and you can really hear it in this track with its fast chromatic runs and daredevil licks.

Around the time of THE YARDBIRDS album two members of the band left; Paul Samwell-Smith and bass player Keith Relf. As a replacement for Relf they hired Jimmy Page as a temporary stand in. Soon afterwards rhythm guitarist Chris Dreja swapped places with Page and The Yardbirds had the first twin lead guitar line-up. They recorded the single *Happenings Ten Years Time Ago* which was the first single to feature dual lead guitar work by Beck and Page.

Photo: David Redfern

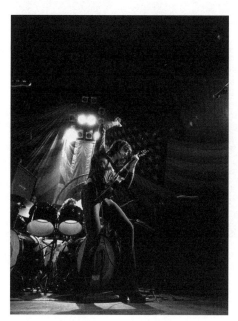

Photo: David Redfern

Beck wasn't happy in The Yardbirds – for some time he had been feeling restricted by the band, and his quick temper flared up on more than one occasion. During a U.S. tour Beck lost his temper on stage and, in a fit of rage, smashed his favourite guitar. Shortly afterwards he flew home and began his solo career.

Jeff's early solo singles were *Love Is Blue* and *Hi Ho Silver Lining/Beck's Bolero*. Although *Hi Ho Silver Lining* is his most well known song and features a rare vocal performance by Beck, it's *Beck's Bolero* that showed the way to his new direction. This song was recorded in two hours and Jeff is accompanied by Jimmy Page and Led Zeppelin bassist John Paul Jones, with The Who's Keith Moon on drums. This line-up was the first incarnation of what was to become Led Zeppelin but Jeff decided to pursue his own band and in late 1967 he formed The Jeff Beck Group with singer Rod Stewart and bassist Ron Wood, who later went on to join The Rolling Stones.

The Band's first album TRUTH is a blues-rock classic with Beck utilising the fuzz-box and wah-wah to great effect. Some of his best early playing can be heard in *I Ain't Superstitious* and a reworking of The Yardbirds' *Shapes Of Things*.

The Jeff Beck Group went on to record the albums BECKOLA and ROUGH AND READY before splitting up in 1972. ROUGH AND READY, which was written and produced by Beck, is more jazz based than the first two, and leads the way for his classic 70s fusion albums BLOW BY BLOW and WIRED. George Martin, the man behind all of those great Beatles recordings, produced both of these albums. Beck surrounded himself with a wealth of talent including Jan Hammer, Max Middleton and Narada Michael Walden. These albums are packed with stunning instrumental virtuosity and musical complexity – intricate rhythms, Beck's seat-of-the-pants guitar style, and great playing from the other musicians all combine to make a definitive musical statement.

During this time Beck contributed a beautiful solo to Stevie Wonder's *Lookin' For Another Pure Love* from the TALKING BOOK album. Interestingly the seminal track *Superstition*, from the same album, was originally written for Beck, but Motown knew a hit when they heard one, and reclaimed the track for Wonder.

Outstanding tracks from this period would have to include *Led Boots* from WIRED and the beautifully lyrical rendition of Stevie Wonder's *Cause We've Ended As Lovers*.

Beck's next solo release THERE AND BACK featured keyboardist Jan Hammer and drummer Simon Phillips – the opening track *Starcycle* was used for years as the theme tune to the U.K. television show 'The Tube'. It's interesting to note that Beck wrote very little of the material on these three great albums, and he has subsequently admitted to feeling intimidated by the musicianship of his bandmates. These were after all some of the best players around at the time. On all of these albums however, over and above the great writing and musicianship of his collaborators, it is Beck's guitar playing that shines brightest. His guitar tone is sometimes delicate and sensitive, sometimes brutal and coarse, and sometimes effected almost beyond recognition – but it's always recognisably Beck.

THERE AND BACK marked the end of Jeff's jazz influenced style. In 1985 he released the album FLASH, a vocal record produced by Chic's Nile Rogers. It had more to do with disco than jazz, though it did give Beck a rare hit with the song *Ambitious*. Around this time Jeff also guested on albums by Tina Turner and Mick Jagger as well as contributing a solo to the Rod Stewart hit *Infatuation*.

Jeff spent the next few years rebuilding his beloved American hot rod cars until the 1989 album GUITAR SHOP. Joined by keyboardist Tony Hymas and ex Frank Zappa

"His style is a unique blend of 50s nostalgia and space-age, high-octane rock"

drummer Terry Bozzio, this album marks a clear return to form for Beck. This instrumental rock-based album includes some great tunes and a variety of outstanding guitar playing ranging from the wildness of *Savoy* to the gorgeous trem-bar manipulated harmonics of *Where Were You*.

In more recent times Jeff has recorded a tribute to his hero Cliff Gallup with an album of Gene Vincent material on CRAZY LEGS and provided the soundtrack to the movie 'Frankie's House'.

Musical Style

Jeff Beck's phenomenal playing has been at the cutting edge of rock since the 60s and has endured to this day. His style is a unique blend of 50s nostalgia and space-age, high-octane rock, fuelled by blues, jazz and a rebellious rock 'n' roll attitude. He has a 'take-no-prisoners' approach to soloing.

Although he's not a technically minded player, and claims to know next to nothing about music theory, he has a command over his instrument that is hard to match, and has created a unique and distinctive style.

Jeff's style really matured in the 70s when he combined his blues and rock influences with jazz and fusion. He would often use simple, repetitive licks over more complex backing tracks in his solos, but his unique phrasing and inventive use of melody always shone through.

His sound is very identifiable, even though he used several guitars through his career. The guitar he is most associated with, though, is the Fender Stratocaster – a guitar that Jeff has used to its maximum potential. On the BLOW BY BLOW album he recorded a version of Charles Mingus' *Goodbye Pork Pie Hat* where he uses all five pickup positions on the Fender Stratocaster.

From the THERE AND BACK album onwards Jeff stopped using a pick and relied on his fingers to do the work. He sometimes pulls on the strings so that they 'snap' back for extra attack. On later albums Jeff used the trem-bar extensively. During WIRED and BLOW BY BLOW he would use the bar to add splashes of colour, like an artist painting with a brush, but by the time of the GUITAR SHOP album he began to play whole tunes just using the bar. The melody on *Three Rivers* from this album is played entirely using harmonics and the trem-bar, and *Where Were You* is also based on this technique.

Photo: Fin Costello

Performance Notes

Jeff's Boogie
This early instrumental appeared on THE YARDBIRDS album but is really a Beck instrumental. The triple-tracked guitar alternates between the chord-based main tune and some flamboyant solo breaks. It's a fast 12/8 that shows the influence on Jeff of 50s rock 'n' roll, especially the Gene Vincent guitarist Cliff Gallup. The multi-tracked harmony guitar is reminiscent of Les Paul.

Musically speaking Beck has never been the bashful type, and he packs a lot of tricks into this guitar showcase. There are fast open string pull-offs, sometimes ascending chromatically, melodies played with harmonics, and blues licks which all return to the same 12 bar chord riff.

The Gene Vincent records that Jeff was brought up on were full of this kind of 'playing on the edge'. Spiced up with a little dissonance here and there, it was a feature of Cliff Gallup's playing that Beck inherited.

Led Boots
Taken from the WIRED album, this track features Beck and Jan Hammer playing head to head, exchanging incendiary solos. This track is a high energy, Indian influenced tune with a real rock feel. The band negotiates the intricate 7/8 bridge sections very smoothly and Jeff's playing throughout is just outstanding, from the

Photo: David Redfern

JEFFBECKdiscography

Photo: Robert Knight

"Musically speaking Beck has never been the bashful type"

opening crashing chords to the most blistering of solos, he plays with real invention and fire.

This tune is riff based with an Indian-influenced riff as the main section, over which Beck plays a bluesy melody line and, later on, a solo. Towards the end Jan Hammer plays a synth solo over the 7/8 bridge riff. Beck uses a range of techniques in this tune from large string bends to rapid trills to trem-bar articulations. And his fuzz-fuelled solo is one of his most exciting on record.

El Becko

This is one of Beck's most harmonically complicated tracks, written by Tony Hymas and Simon Phillips. Taken from the THERE AND BACK album, the intro features Hymas' piano skills as he plays fast arpeggios that lead into an almost orchestral sounding section with Jeff playing a high melody. The main tune is a D minor, blues-based guitar riff that is followed by a slide guitar melody in A. The straightforward rock harmony of these sections contrasts well with the more harmonically complex parts.

The solo is typical of Beck's aggressive style with fast flurries of notes and double string bends raising the excitement level through the roof!

Although Beck is an accomplished slide player, this is one of his few performances on record. In later years he mastered the art of faking slide with his trem-bar.

Starcycle

With Jan Hammer on keyboard, writing and drumming duties, this track brought Beck into the high-tech 80s. The bass sequence that runs throughout the track and Hammer's synth soloing add a 'futuristic' element to Beck's guitar.

Jeff's playing is as inspired as always, and more disciplined than on his earlier albums. The whole tune has a tight, well arranged feel with Beck's solo adding a welcome dose of abandon.

The main melody is doubled with a second guitar and keyboards and on the repeats with one guitar playing a fifth higher. The solo is played over a four chord sequence, which restricts Jeff's playing a little, but he still manages to get in some trills, trem-bar dives and furious string bends.

Savoy

The GUITAR SHOP album that this track came from marks a move away from the jazz-fusion of WIRED and THERE AND BACK. With the aid of Terry Bozzio's industrial-sounding drums and Tony Hymas' sophisticated and subtle chord work, Beck creates a rock shuffle for the space age. This, more than any track, encapsulates his style, from the 50s tinged triple string bends of the main riff to high-tech trem-bar articulations. In the bridge you can hear Beck's trademark trills which he bends up with the bar.

In the intro he plays a repeated low E string that sounds like half-harmonic half-machinery! Remember that by this time he was playing almost exclusively without a pick and the action of repeatedly plucking the low string with his fingers produces these half harmonics. This imaginative use of simple ideas is typical of Beck.

Just before the solo starts he plays a series of high, sliding harmonics produced by lightly touching the bottom string and sliding from the second to the fourth fret whilst playing a rhythm pattern with his picking hand.

Big Block

The title refers to the muscle cars that Beck spends his spare time rebuilding when he's not churning out a down and dirty blues like this. The guitar is fairly sparse at the start of this track with Beck providing some Delta-style blues guitar over the massive drum groove. In the bridge he plays a more familiar role as the distorted guitar kicks in.

There are some tricky time changes in the bridge section where the syncopations at the end of the bar become the down-beat of the next bar.

The solo is a tour de force of modern rock techniques as Jeff using pick-hand taps for trills and trem-bar phrasing with harmonics culminating in a frenzied tapping/sliding lick.

Tablature Key

Hammer-on

Play the first note with one finger then 'hammer' another finger on the fret indicated.

Pull-off

Place both fingers on the notes to be sounded, play the first note and, without picking, pull the finger off to sound the lower note.

Gliss

Play the first note and then slide the same fret-hand finger up or down to the second note. Don't strike the second note.

Gliss and restrike

Same as legato slide, except the second note is struck.

Quarter-tone bend

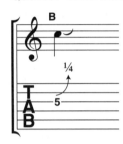

Play the note then bend up a quarter-tone.

Half-tone bend

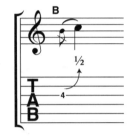

Play the note then bend up a semi-tone.

Whole-tone bend

Play the note then bend up a whole-tone.

Bend of more than a tone

Play the note then bend up as required.

Bend and return

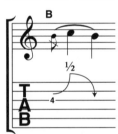

Play the note, bend up as indicated, then return back to the original note.

Compound bend and return

Play the note then bend up and down in the rhythm shown.

Pre-bend

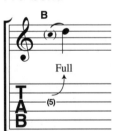

Bend the note as shown before striking.

Pre-bend and return

Bend the note as shown before striking it, then return it back to its original pitch.

Unison bend

Play the two notes together and bend the lower note up to the pitch of the higher one.

Double stop bend and return

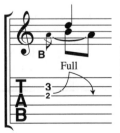

Hold the top note, then bend and return the bottom notes on a lower string.

Bend and tap

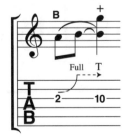

Bend the note as shown and tap the higher fret while still holding the bend.

Vibrato

Rapidly bend and release the note with the fretting hand.

Trill

Rapidly alternate between the notes indicated by continuously hammering on and pulling off.

Tapping

Hammer ('tap') the fret indicated with the pick-hand index or middle finger and pull off the note fretted by the fret-hand.

Pick scrape

The edge of the pick is rubbed along the string, producing a scratchy sound.

Muffled strings

Lay the fret-hand lightly across the strings then play with the pick-hand.

Natural harmonic

Play the note while the fret-hand lightly touches the string directly over the fret indicated.

Pinch harmonic

Fret the note normally and produce a harmonic by adding the edge of the thumb or the tip of the index finger of the pick hand to the normal pick attack.

Arpeggiate

Play the notes of the chord by rolling them in the direction of the arrow.

Palm muting

Allow the pick-hand to rest lightly on the strings whilst playing.

Rake

Drag the pick across the strings shown with a single motion.

Tremolo picking

Repeatedly pick the note as rapidly as possible.

Vibrato-bar slur

Slightly depress bar then play the note and release the bar to slur up to pitch.

Vibrato-bar bend

Play the first note then pull up or push down on the vibrato-bar to the pitch of the second note.

Vibrato-bar dive and return

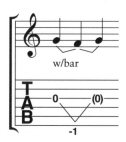

Drop the pitch of the note or chord a specific number of steps (in rhythm) then return to the original pitch.

Vibrato-bar dips

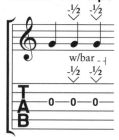

Play the first note then use the bar to drop a specific number of steps, then release back to the original pitch, in rhythm. Only the first note is picked.

Savoy

Words and Music by Jeff Beck, Tony Hymas and Terry Bozzio

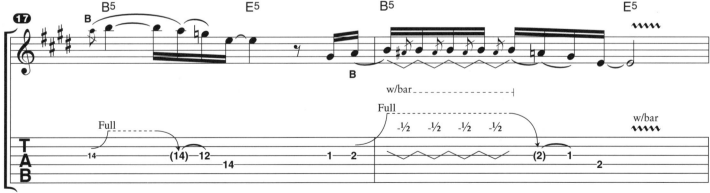

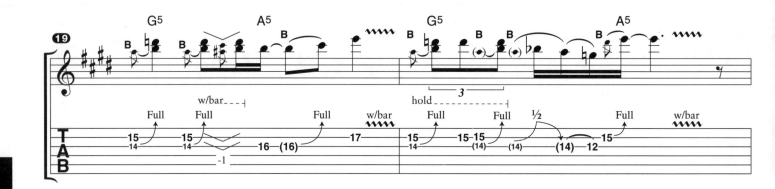

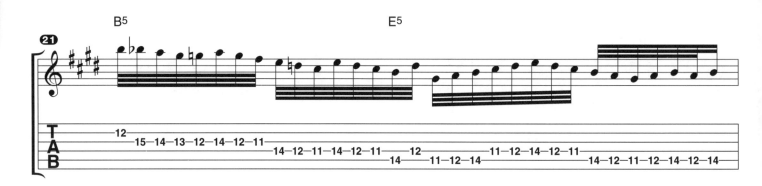

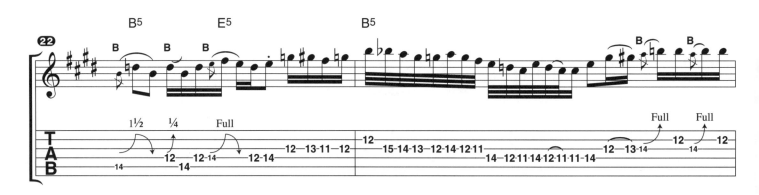

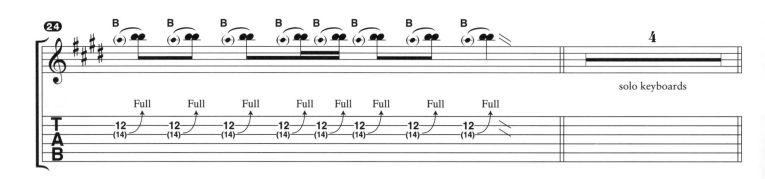

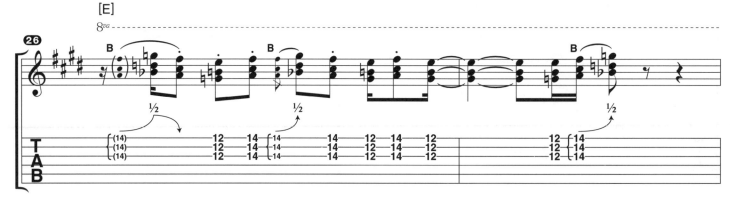

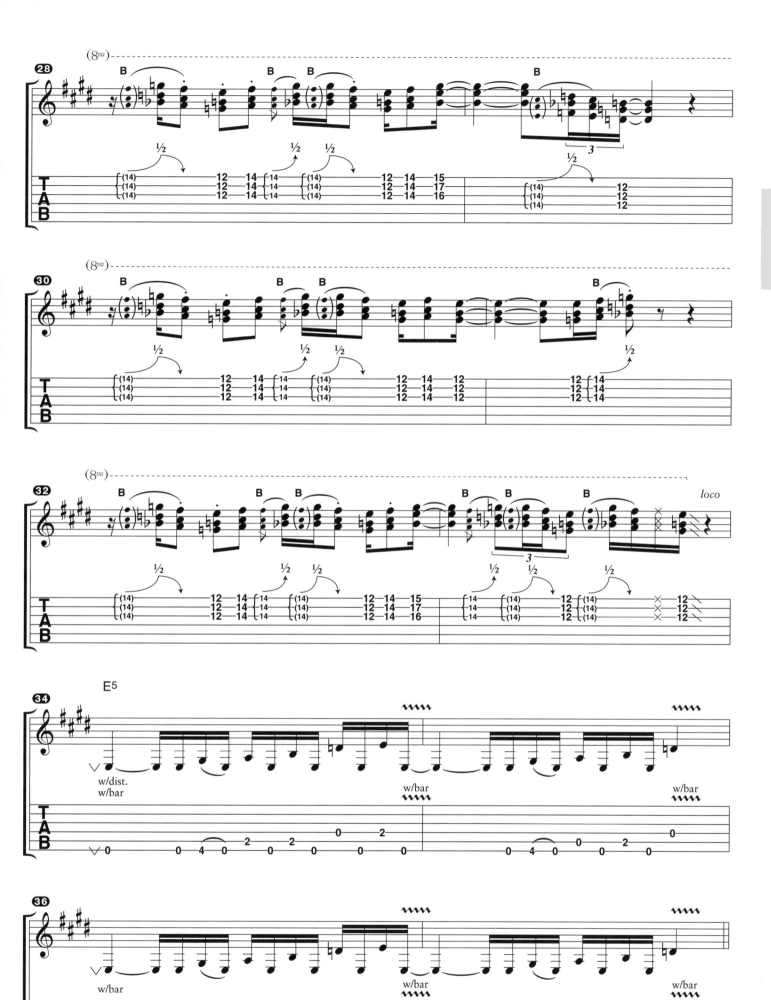

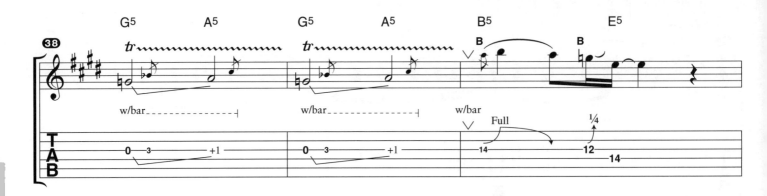

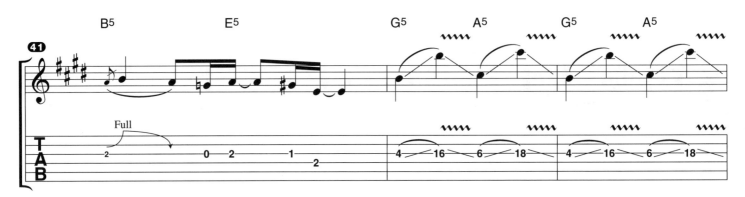

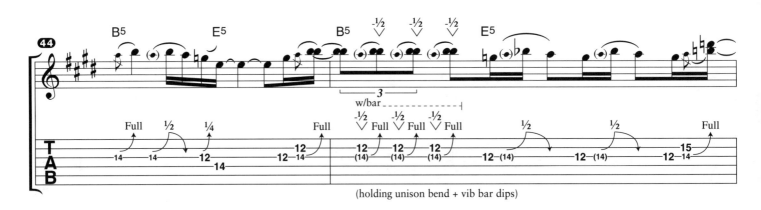

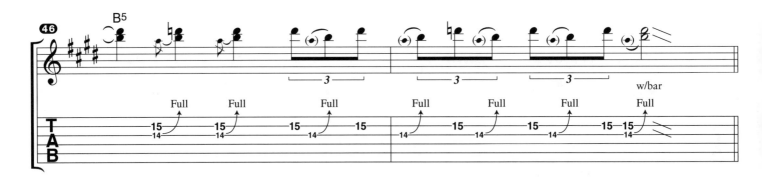

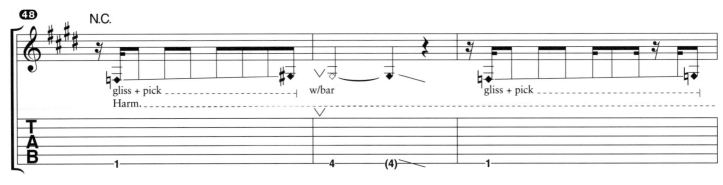

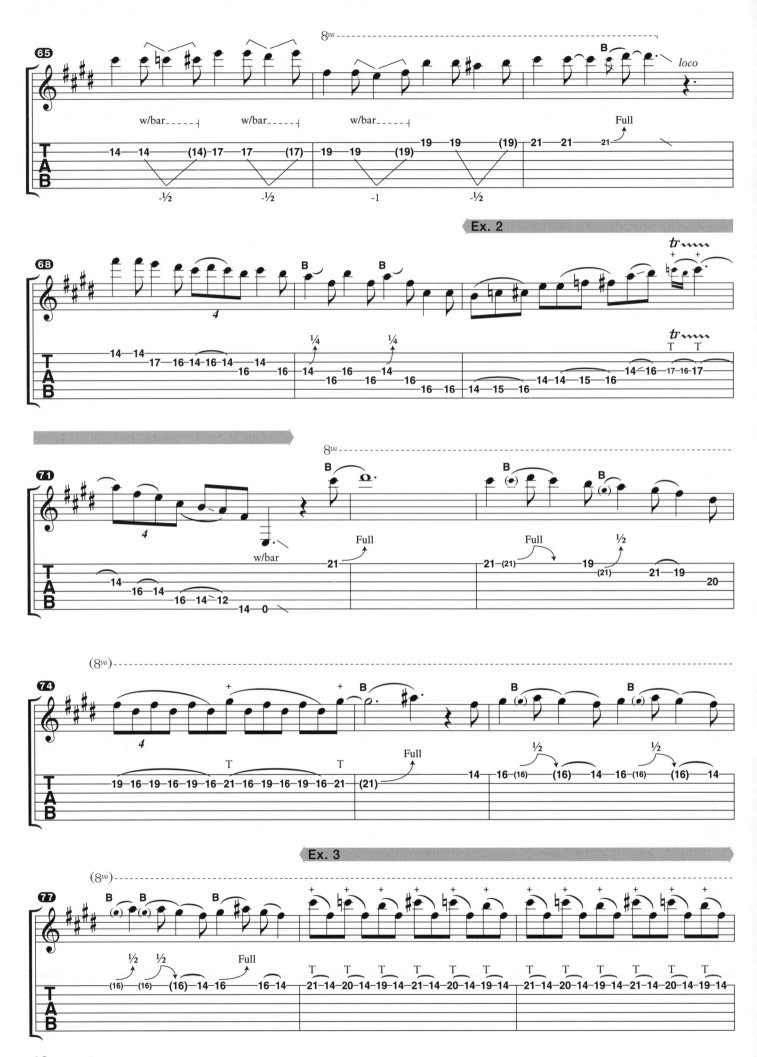

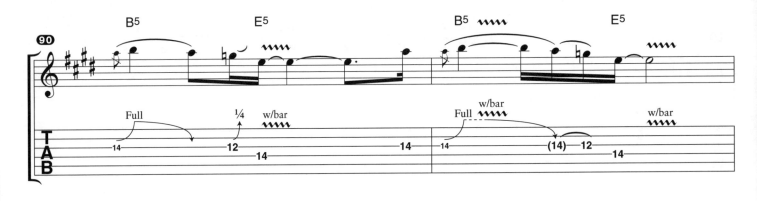

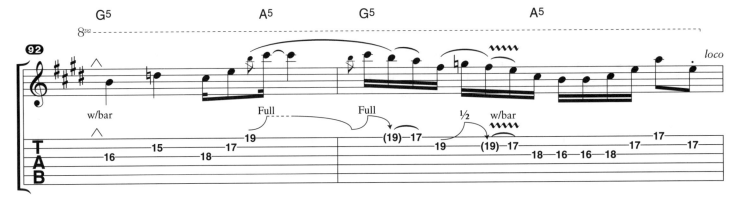

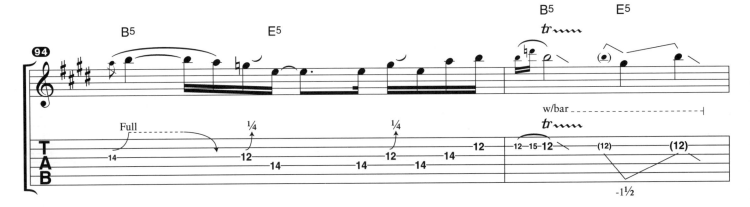

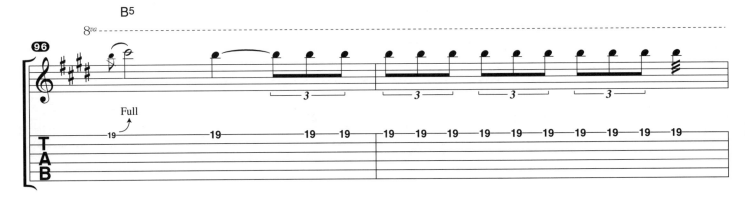

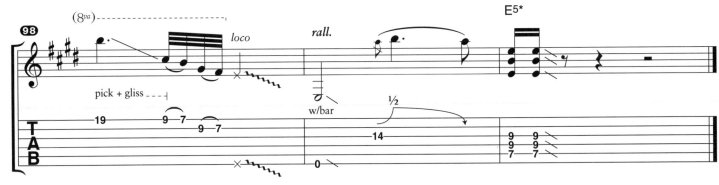

The Solo

Savoy

Throughout this mid-tempo rock shuffle Beck uses a host of unusual techniques as he strives to wrench every possible sound from his guitar. This is Beck playing at his best and, ably supported by Bozzio and Hymas, he reaches new heights of pyrotechnic guitar expertise.

Ex 1

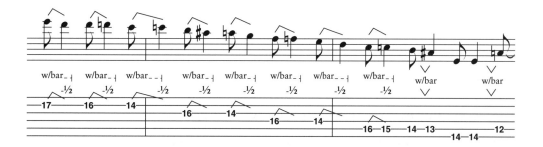

Jeff is a master at mimicking the sound of slide guitar and harmonica. To do this he uses his trem-bar to slur some of the notes together. To get the sound of a harmonica he rolls down the tone control on his guitar, which, in addition to picking with the pads of his fingers, softens the attack of the notes.

You'll need to hold the trem-bar as you play this phrase, and this is easier if you pick with your fingers as Jeff does. Every other note in this descending, chromatic line is played by dropping the pitch with the trem-bar. You have

to be very accurate with the pitch as the movement is only a semi-tone.

Ex 2

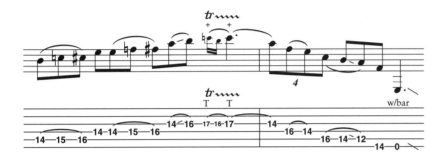

There are a few examples of pick-hand tapping in this solo. In this example Jeff uses the technique to play a fast semi-tone trill in the middle of a bluesy run.

The ascending lick should be played with your first three fingers. When you get to the G string, slide up with your first finger to the B note and tap with your picking hand on the C a semi-tone above.

This is a very fast trill and to get out of it requires some nifty finger work. Just before the second bar, as you are tapping with your pick-hand, move down from the B note to an A with your first finger, and pull-off the tapped note to it. This all happens very fast but it is quite easy to do.

Ex 3

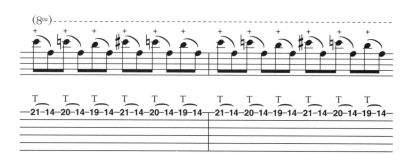

This is another tapping lick, but this time using an interesting cross-rhythm. Hold down the F♯ with your first finger and tap the chromatic descending line with your pick-hand.

The two note pattern creates a shifting rhythmic pattern over the 12/8 backing.

Make sure you keep your tapping hand relaxed as you pull-off to keep the rhythm steady. It's easy to get a lop-sided feel when using this technique.

TECHNIQUEtip

If you feel that you're playing is in a rut, throw away that pick and play like a man! Picking with your fingers will slow you down and make you think more about phrasing and melody

Ex 4

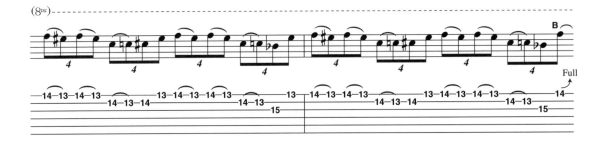

This is a very fast lick that will need some practice to get it up to speed. There are times in a solo when Beck raises the energy through the roof with a frenzy of notes and this is one of those times.

The shape and fingering of this lick is the same for the top two strings. You can see a repeating pattern emerge if you play slowly through it. Use your first and second fingers on the B and E strings and let your third finger cover the G string.

The lick is neatly arranged into four-note groups which will help you to play the correct rhythm up to speed.

STARCYCLE

Words and Music by Jan Hammer

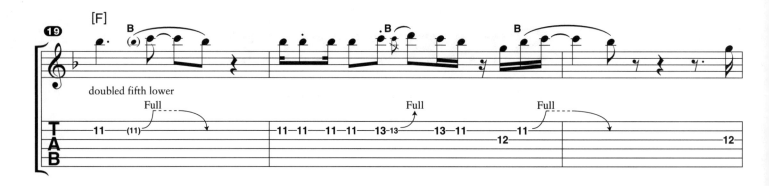

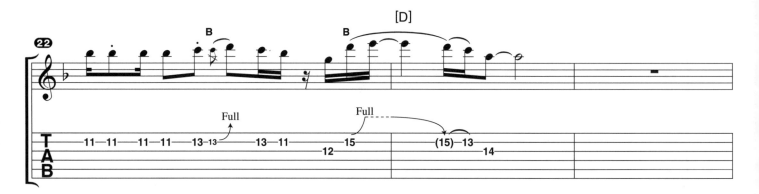

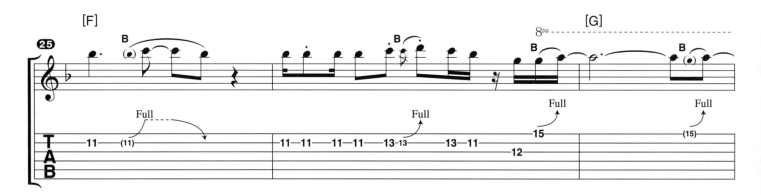

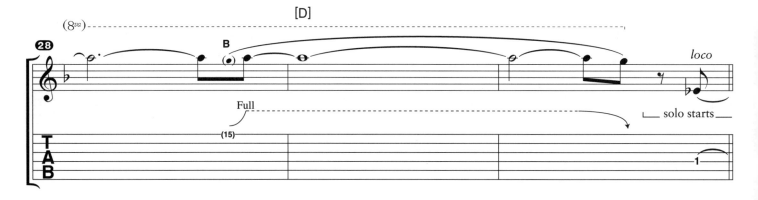

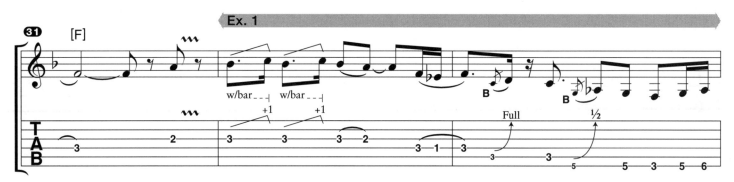

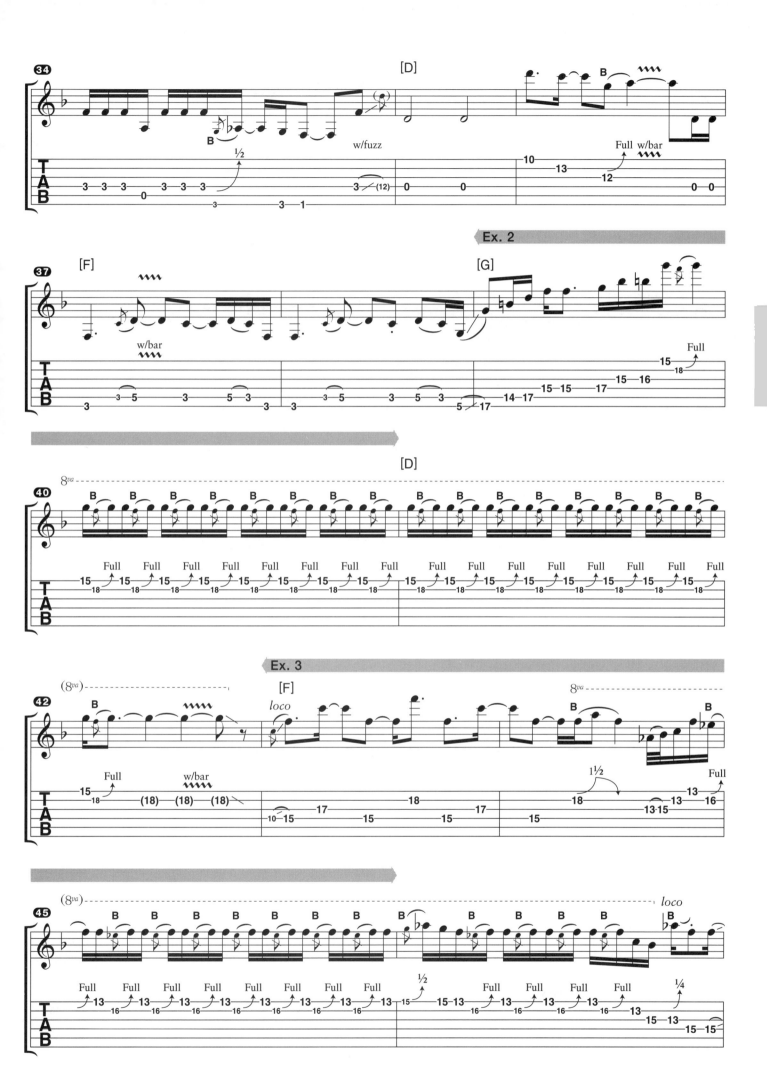

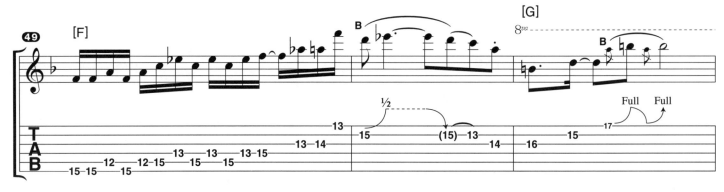

Ex. 4

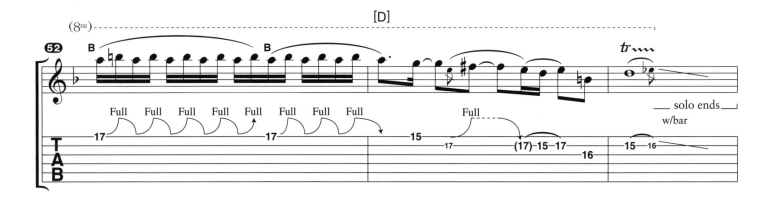

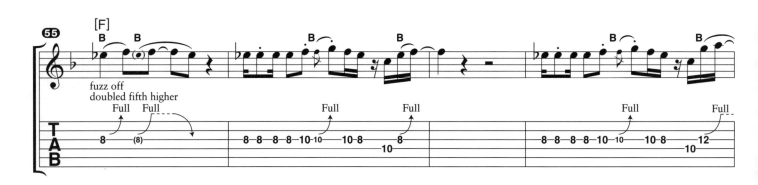

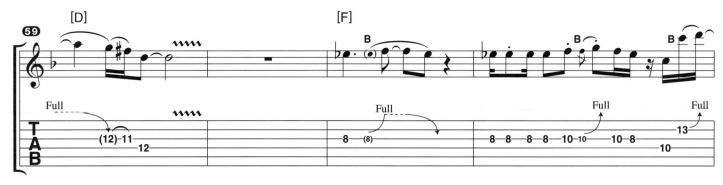

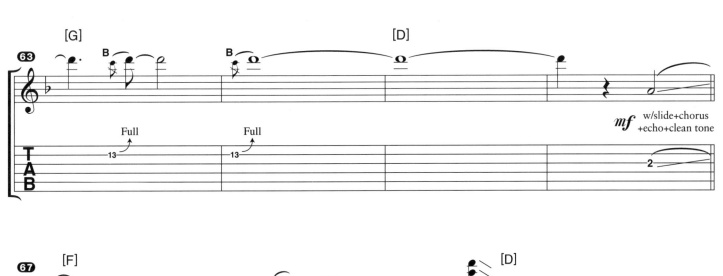

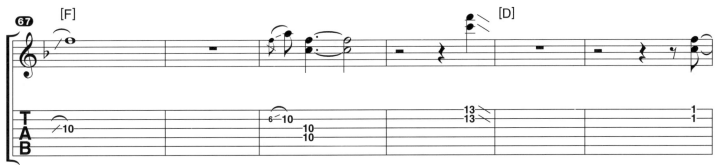

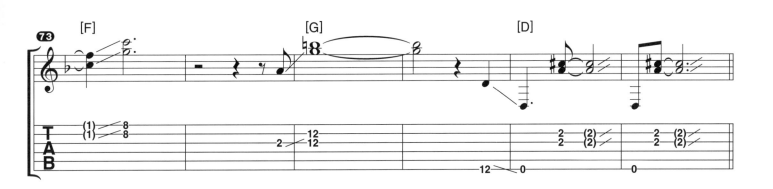

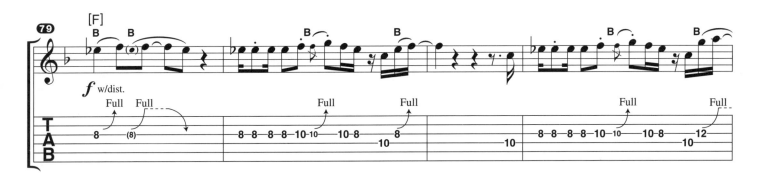

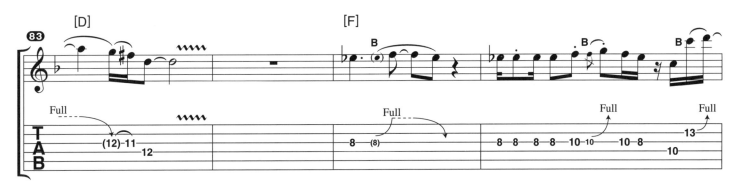

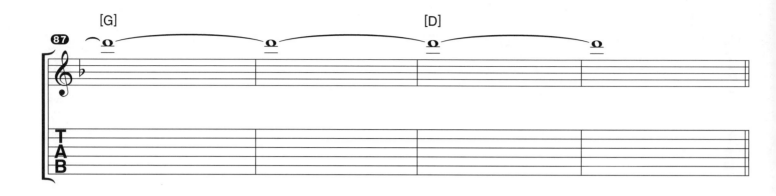

Synth solo arr. for gtr.

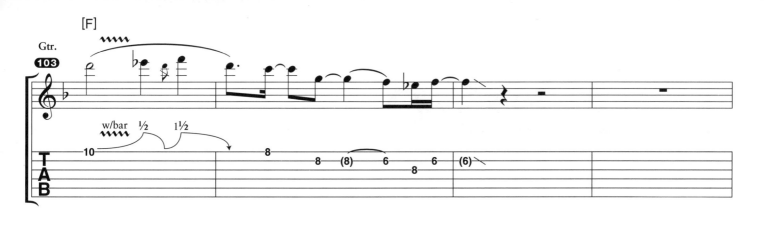

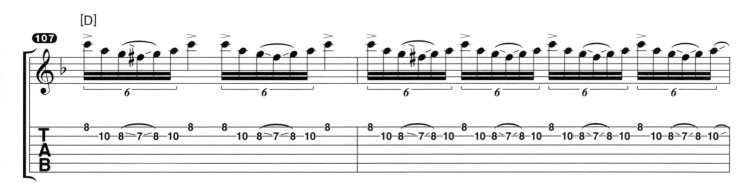

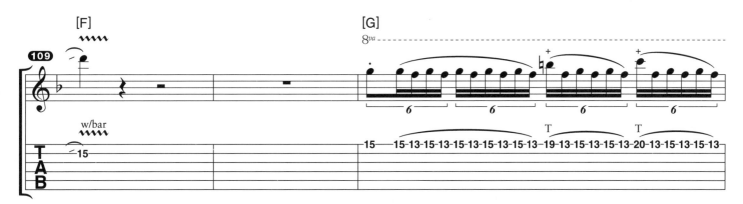

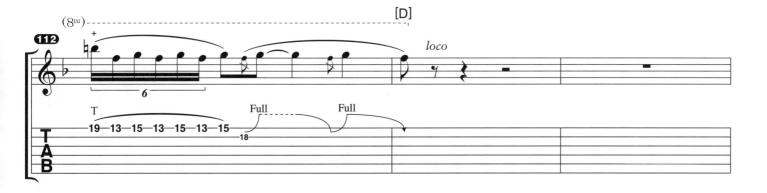

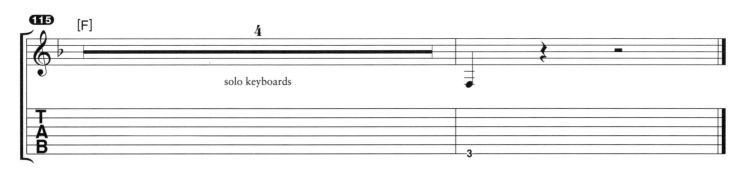

The Solo

Starcycle

Taken from the album THERE AND BACK this Jan Hammer penned track features keyboards heavily. Jeff Beck, however, is not the type to take a back seat, and his soloing is as energetic as ever.

This track is based around an implied four-chord sequence, and Jeff has to navigate his way through these changes. This has an effect on the structure of this solo, as Jeff establishes the sound of each chord before taking off into the stratosphere.

Ex 1

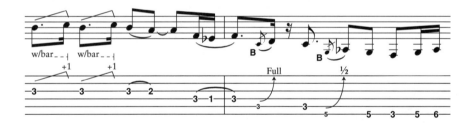

By the time of THERE AND BACK Beck was beginning to use the trem-bar in more innovative ways. In this lick he uses the bar to bend from B♭ to C on the G string. Although he could easily have played this with a string

bend, using the bar has a different, more metallic sound. Jeff has always had his Fender Stratocaster's trem-bar setup with some up-lift, so that he can pull up on the strings to raise their pitch.

Ex 2

Jeff's playing over a G7 tonality here, and he sets up the chord with a matching arpeggio in the first bar. In the second bar he plays a trademark repeating bend lick that overlaps onto the D chord. Although this lick wouldn't work on its own over a D, by setting it up over the G chord he has created a nice tension that he resolves skilfully in the next bar.

For the G7 arpeggio, start with your second finger on the bottom string. You can use your first and third fingers for the rest of the arpeggio until you reach the G string. As with the other string bending licks, use your first finger on the high string and your third finger, supported by one or two others, on the lower one.

Ex 3

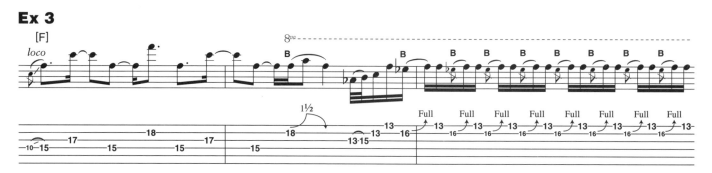

When the chord progression returns to F, Beck spells out
the tonality by playing this three note pattern of F and C.
Here again he's used a syncopated rhythm to breath life
into the simple melodic idea. Once the sound of the chord
is established he takes off into another bending lick that's
similar to the one in Ex 2. This kind of re-working of ideas
helps to create a cohesive, structured solo.

For the phrase in the first bar you can
hold down one shape using your first,
third and fourth fingers, then use your
third finger to play the large bend in the
second bar.

TECHNIQUEtip

Sooner or later you'll have to
play over more complex chord
changes, and it needn't be a
problem. When you begin
make sure your phrases start
and end on chord tones. You'll
soon find yourself playing
through even the most
challenging changes, then, as
you become more confident
you can start to use non-
chord tones

Ex 4

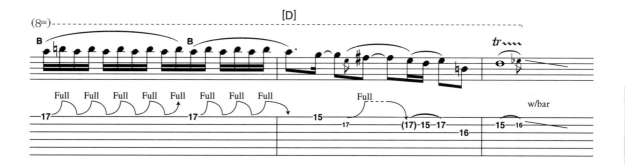

In the final bars of the solo Jeff plays a repeated whole tone bend on the top string followed by a more melodic phrase in the second bar that resolves the whole solo to D.

The bends, as usual, are played with a supported third finger. Make sure you release the bend completely to get the full 'see-saw' effect of this lick.

In the last bar of the solo he plays another of his flashy semi-tone trills, but this time he drops the pitch of the string as he plays it to create a dive-bombing trill effect.

BIG BLOCK

Words and Music by Jeff Beck, Tony Hymas and Terry Bozzio

*Chords implied by harmony

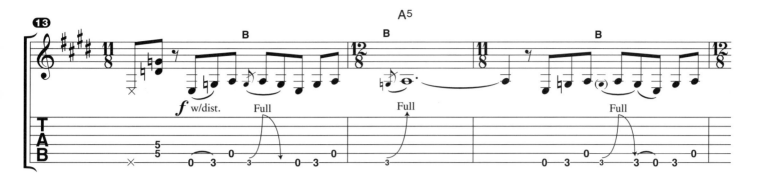

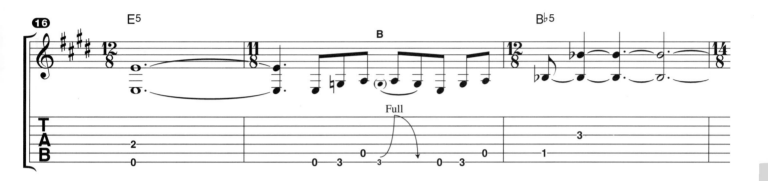

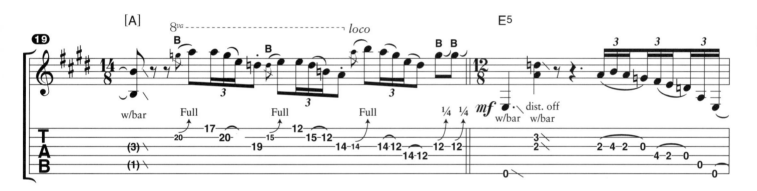

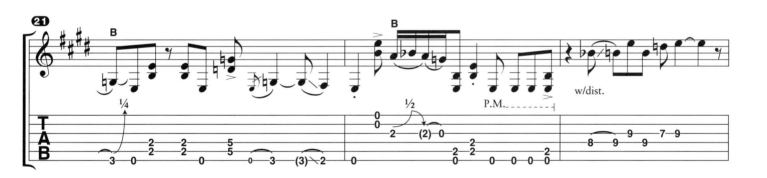

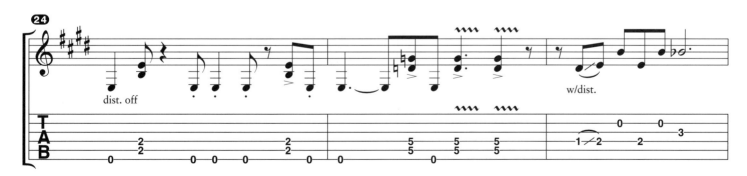

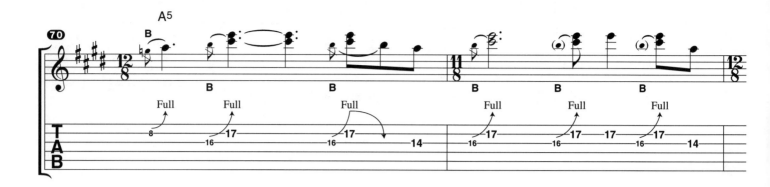

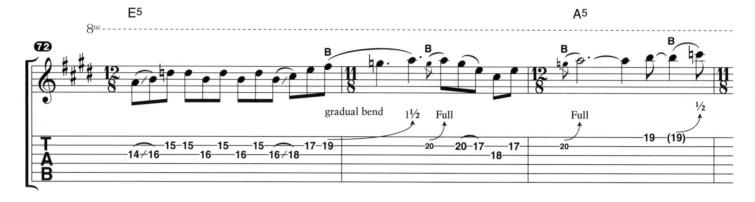

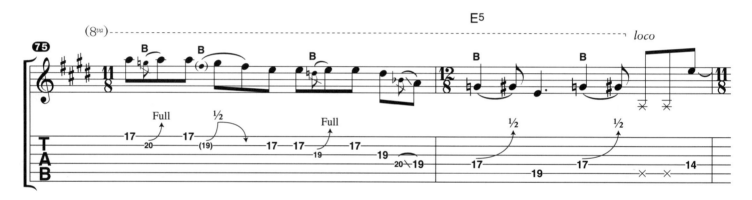

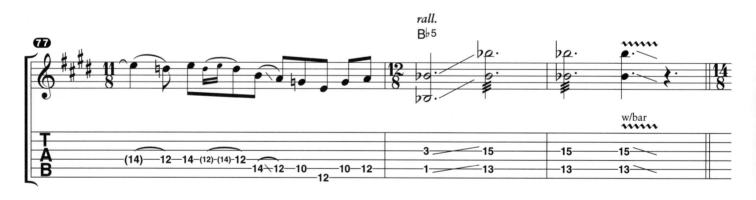

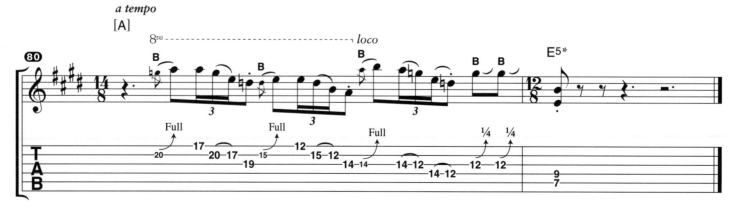

The Solo

Big Block

This solo is probably Beck's most technically accomplished on record. There are modern rock guitar techniques everywhere, from fast tapped trills and trem-bar swoops to pinched harmonics. That's not to say that Beck has lost touch with his blues roots, as his playing is as earthy and gutsy as ever.

Ex 1

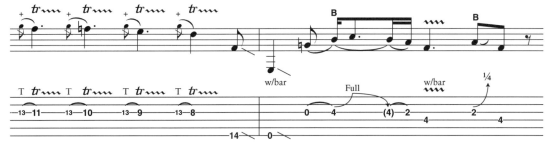

This is the first of many tapping licks in this solo. In this one the tapping hand stays on the same note and trills, while the other hand descends chromatically.

You can use your first finger to play the whole of the descending line – it will help keep the trill constant – or you can use more fingers. It doesn't matter as long as you end up on the first finger, so that your third finger is free to

play the gliss down the E string.

In the second bar use your third finger to hammer-on from the open G string to the B note, then bend up to C♯ in one movement.

The vibrato on the F♯ is heavy and should be done with the trem-bar.

Ex 2

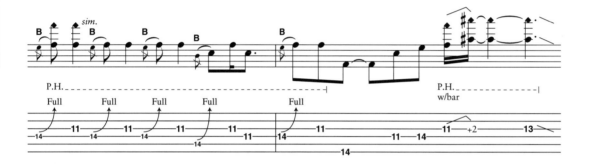

The whole of this lick is played using pinch-harmonics. If you use a pick you would play these by hitting the string with the pick and the flesh of the thumb at the same time. Jeff does a similar thing but uses his first finger instead of a pick. Aim for a ZZ-Top style half harmonic throughout the lick.

The final note in the second bar is pulled up two tones using the trem-bar. If you don't have your guitar set this way you can get the same effect by using a string bend – just remember to use three fingers to bend the string.

Ex 3

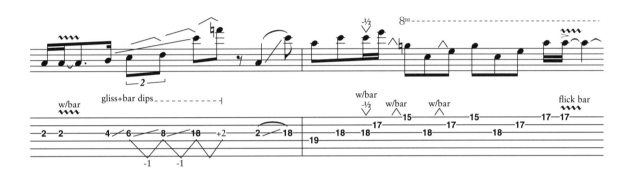

This lazy sounding, ascending lick is played using a combination of two techniques: trem-bar dips and glissando.

From the B note use your first finger to slide up to C♯, D♯ and a high C♯. Each time you slide up, simultaneously press down then release the trem-bar. Only the first note is picked. After the long slide up to the high C♯ use the bar again to pull the note up two tones.

In the second bar Beck uses the trem-bar to slur into some of the notes. To play these slurs press down slightly on the bar, no more than a semi-tone, and play the note as you release the bar. At the end of this bar you can hear a fluttering effect on the last note. This is done by 'flicking' the trem-bar so that it vibrates as you hold the note.

Ex 4

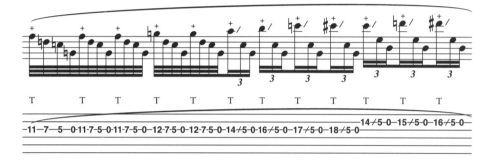

This final frenzied lick looks far more difficult than it is. Start by playing the tapping lick in the normal way, with your fretting hand pulling off to the open string. As your tapping hand starts to ascend add quick slides up the string. You now have to tap the note and quickly gliss up towards the top of the neck, pull-off to your fretting hand's first finger then pull this off to the open string.

Once you've established the pattern it's really quite easy. Don't worry too much about the actual notes, just go for the effect of zipping those notes into orbit.

TECHNIQUEtip

Beck often uses the trem-bar to slur notes in a phrase. It's a great sound that can liven up even the most simple phrase. Try playing some of your favourite licks with trem-bar slurs. You may start to see the guitar in a whole new light!

LED BOOTS

Words and Music by Max Middleton

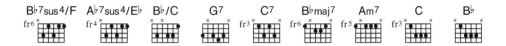

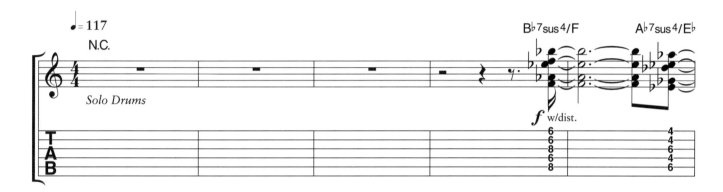

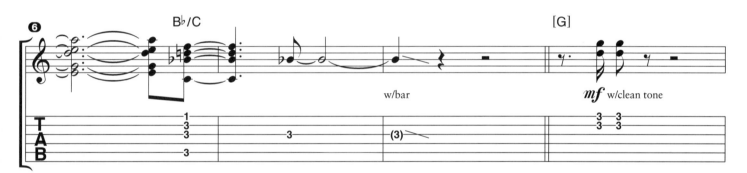

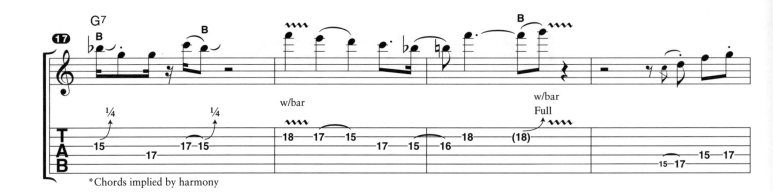

*Chords implied by harmony

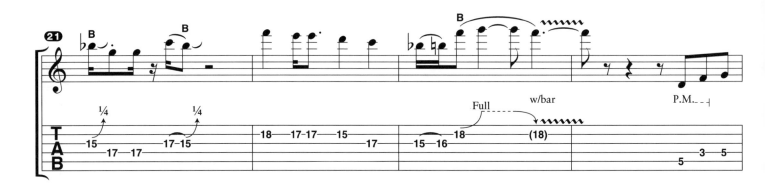

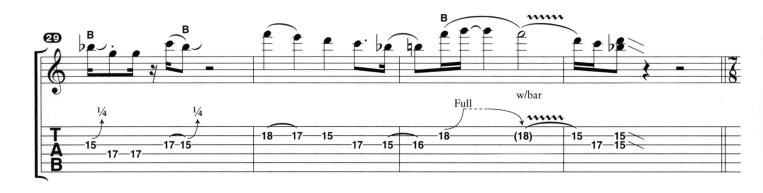

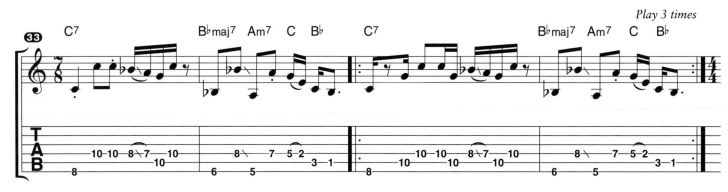

46   *Led Boots*

Ex. 4

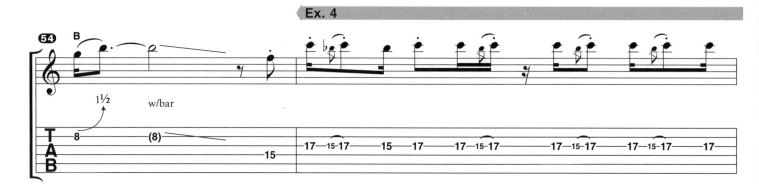

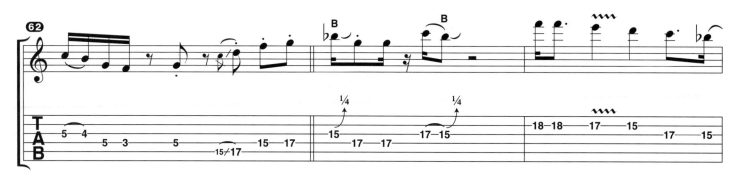

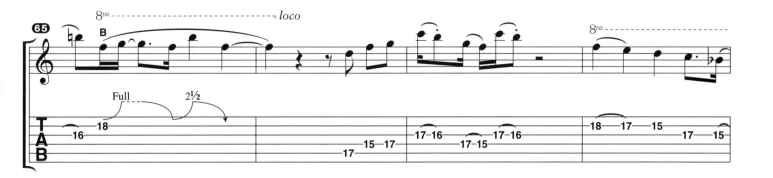

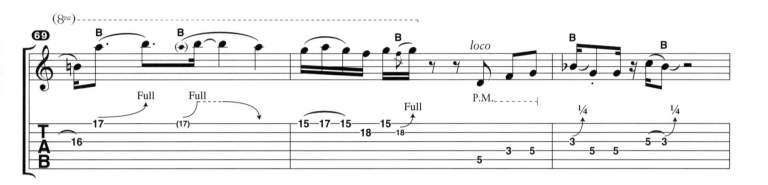

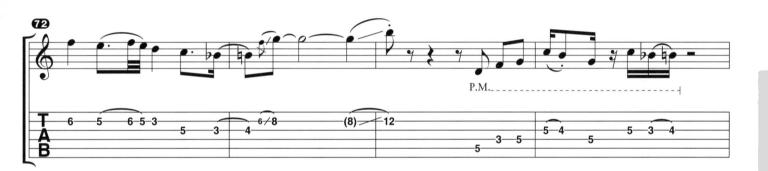

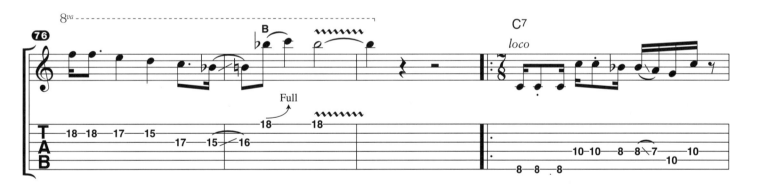

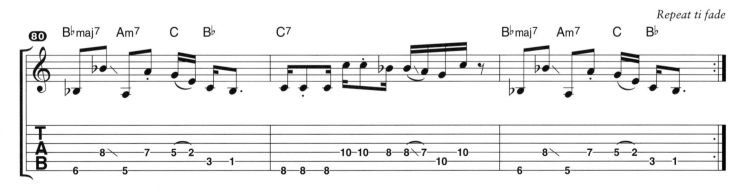

The Solo

Led Boots

A good Jeff Beck solo should sound raw and unleashed, and this is one of his best. Jeff picks up on the high-energy drumming of Narada Michael Walden and takes it to an even higher level in this solo.

You can get a good insight into Beck's style here – the musical material he's using is straightforward enough, but the way he uses it is breathtaking. There is a raw, muscular feel to the string bends and vibrato; Beck is a very 'physical' player who isn't afraid to manhandle his instrument, as you can tell by the way he practically wrenches sounds from his guitar.

Ex 1

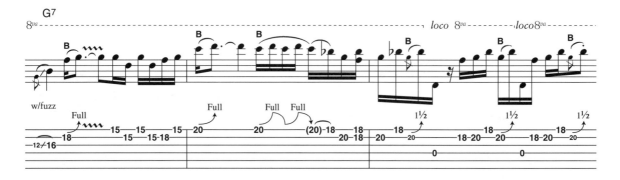

This is a very bold start to a solo – a real statement of axe-wielding intent. The opening high bend has heavy vibrato on it, possibly from his trem-bar. In the second bar he uses

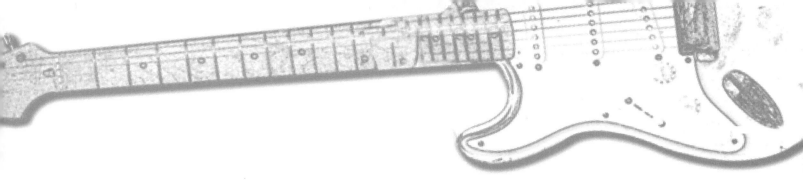

rhythmic string bending, playing the repeating bend to a strict rhythm. Play these bends with your third finger, supporting it with the first and second. Make sure you release the bend fully before re-bending back up to the D note.

Another of Beck's trademark sounds is his use of large string bends. In the third bar he uses a 1½ bend from G to B♭. Although the difference between this and a normal bend is very slight, it adds that element of excitement and feels great to play. Once again make sure to support your bending finger.

Ex 2

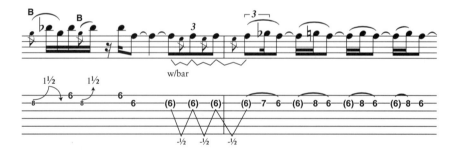

Jeff uses more wide bends here as well as some trem-bar 'dips'. As you may have noticed by now, it's very rare for Beck just to hold a note without doing something to it. As he holds the F note in the first bar over into the second he first manipulates it with the trem before using a G♭ as a repeating grace note. Beck will often trill semitones even if the note he is trilling with is not in the key of the song, as here. He just likes the extra spice this adds. The slightly ragged feel and slower pace of this lick provides a breathing space before he launches into the rest of the solo.

Ex 3

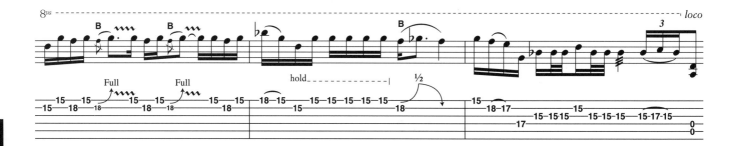

We're back up at the 15th fret now as Beck plays another repeating bend lick, this time using normal bends. Notice the heavy vibrato on the bent notes – you should try to make a feature of this.

At the start of the second bar use your first finger to barre across the top two strings, so that the D note keeps ringing as you play the G on the top string

Ex 4

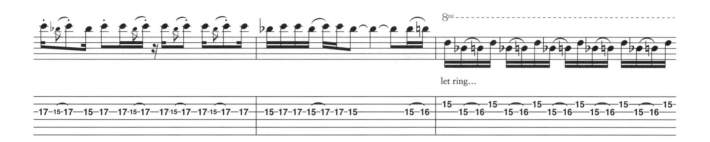

let ring...

Beck's imaginative use of simple ideas is one of his strongest musical assets. Here you can see him using a simple two-note lick, combined with a syncopated rhythm, to make an interesting phrase, which he then expands into a new phrase in the third bar. Use a first finger barre across the G and B strings at this point, and play the hammer-ons with your second finger.

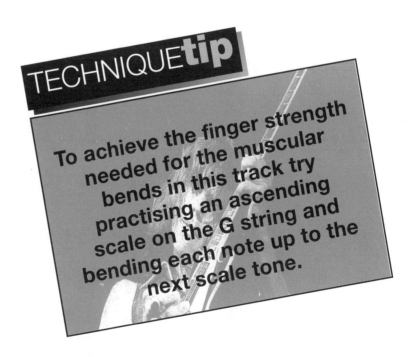

TECHNIQUE**tip**

To achieve the finger strength needed for the muscular bends in this track try practising an ascending scale on the G string and bending each note up to the next scale tone.

JEFF'S BOOGIE

Words and Music by Jeff Beck

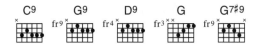

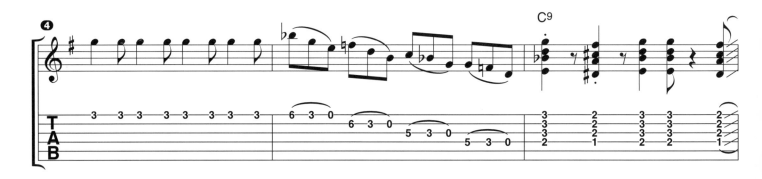

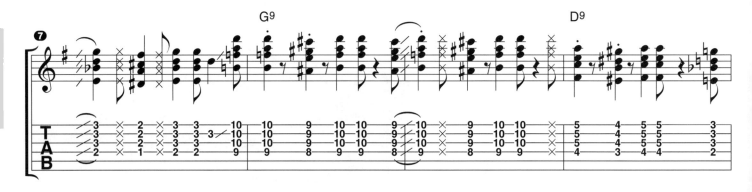

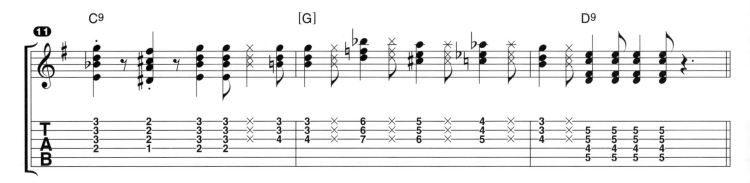

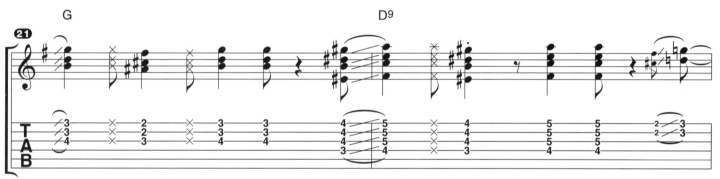

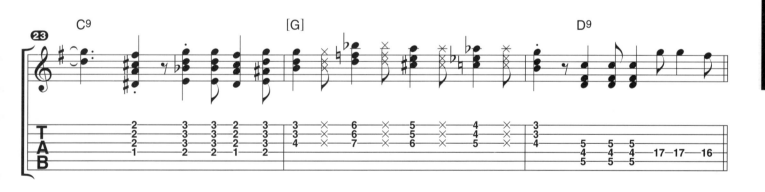

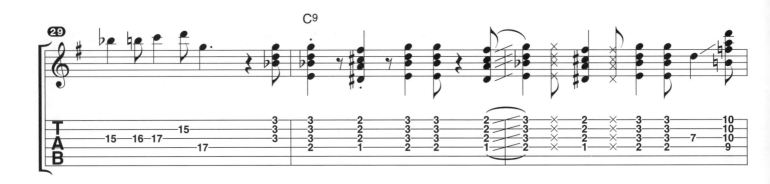

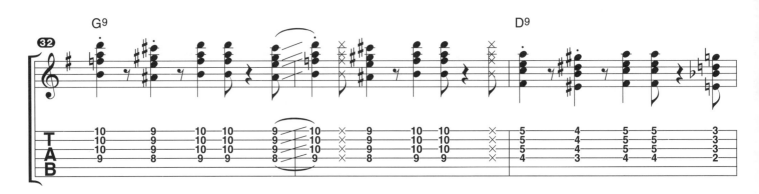

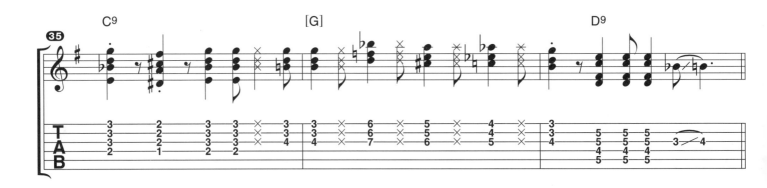

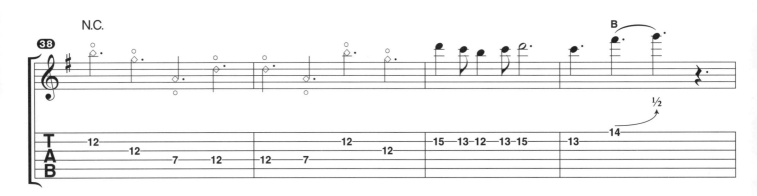

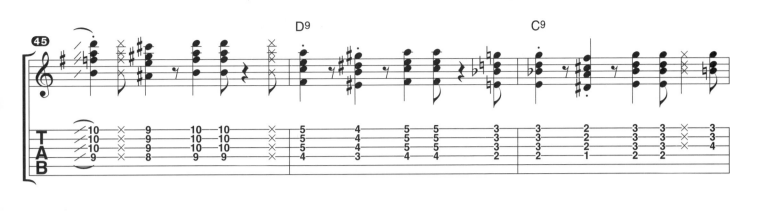

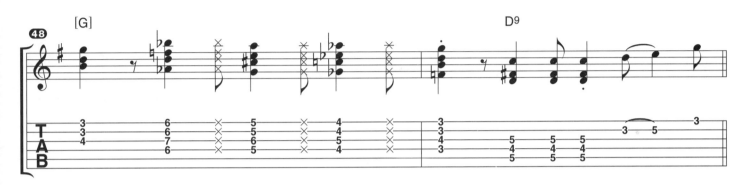

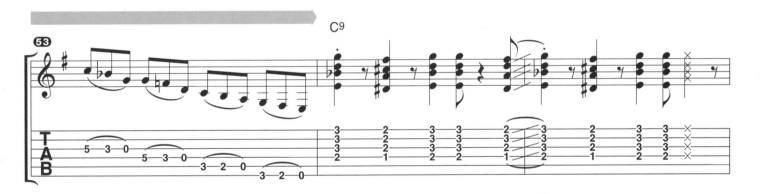

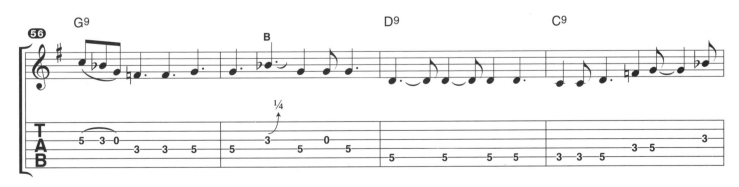

Ex. 2

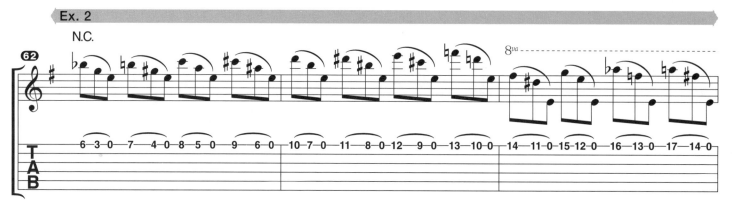

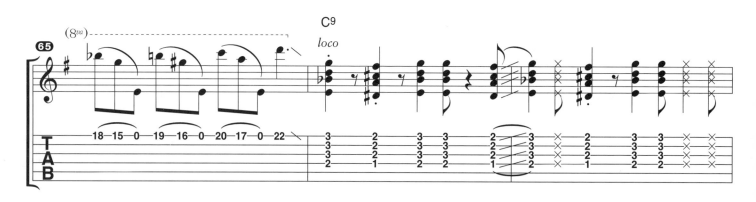

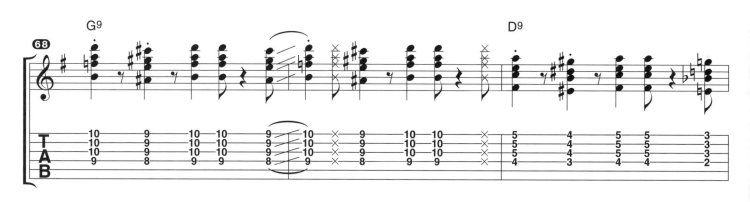

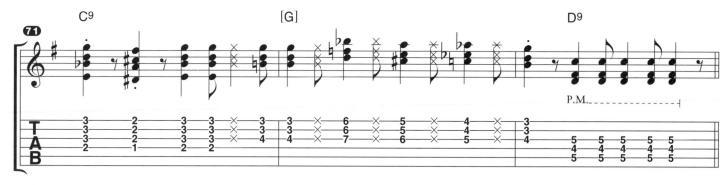

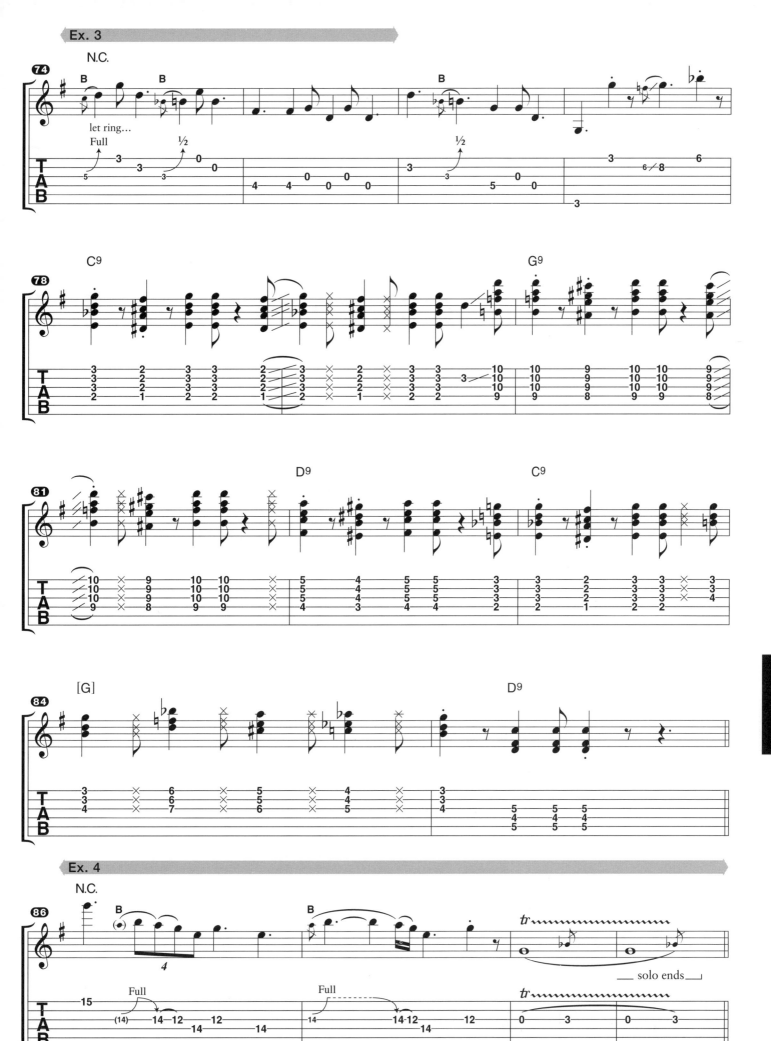

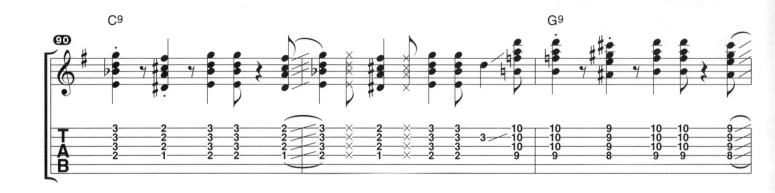

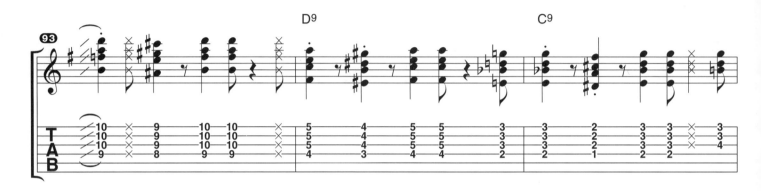

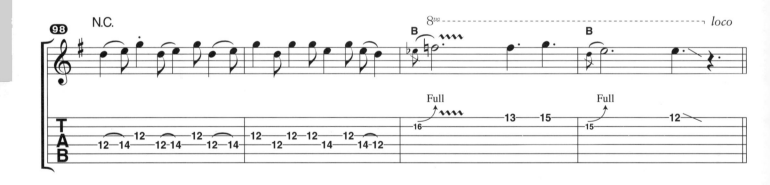

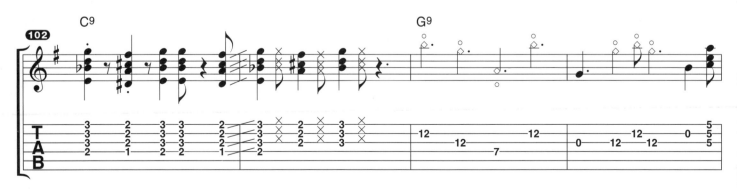

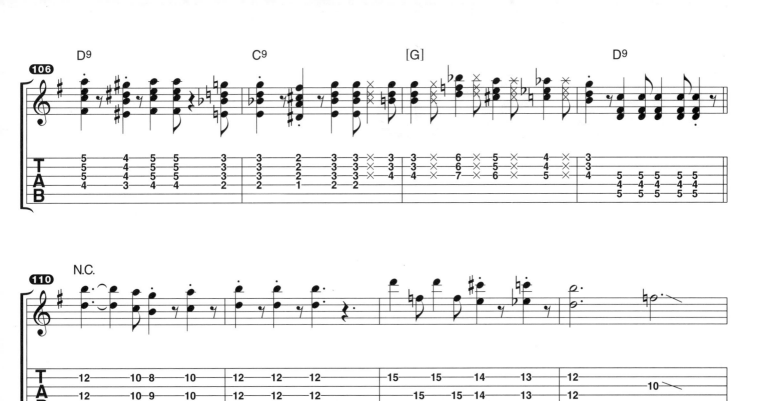

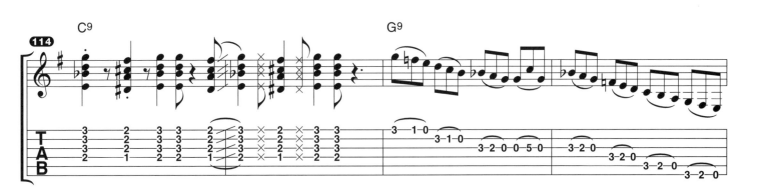

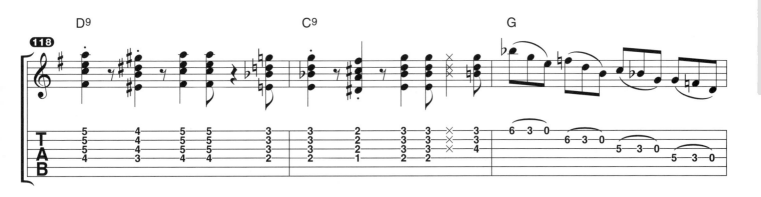

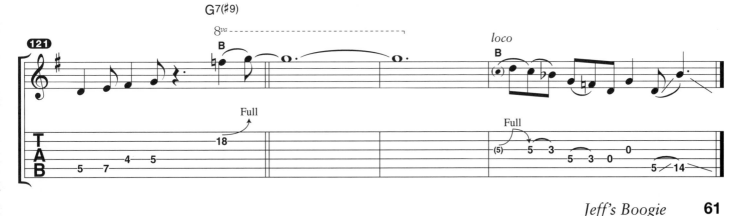

The Solo

Jeff's Boogie

This is a great tribute to the rockabilly and western swing styles of Cliff Gallup and Les Paul. You can hear the Les Paul influence in the multi-tracked harmony parts, and those fast and furious open string pull-offs are pure Gallup. Jeff adds his own style to this track too: the high-energy approach and that feeling that he's playing right at the edge, just in control, are trademark Beck.

The tune revolves around a 12 bar chord riff in G with Jeff using the top four strings to play the G9, C9 and D9 chords.

Ex 1

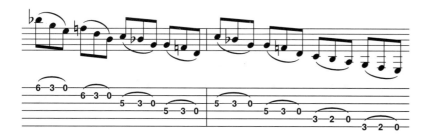

This is the first of two pull-off licks in this tune. It's based around a G pentatonic scale shape but the addition of the open strings adds notes outside the scale. This creates a semi-dissonant sound that is very effective, especially as

these notes zip by so fast, creating a fleetingly dissonant flavour.

The easiest way to play this lick is to use the same fingering for all strings. Start with the third finger, then pull-off to your first finger before pulling-off again to the open string. As an alternative you could use your fifth finger instead of the third on the top two strings.

Ex 2

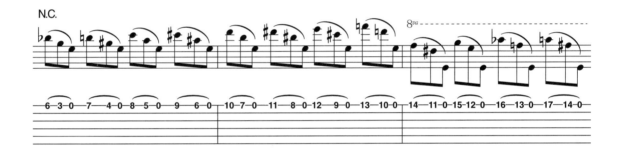

In this lick Beck uses a similar idea to Ex 1, but instead of moving across the strings he moves the shape chromatically up the top string.

Use the same fingering as before but make sure you pick the first note of each three-note group cleanly. This will be more difficult as this lick is all on one string, so you'll have to co-ordinate your two hands exactly to get a clean attack.

Ex 3

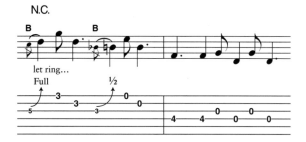

The secret of success in this lick is to keep all the strings ringing as long as possible. At the end of the first bar you have a ½ bend from B♭ to B. Play this with your first finger and arch it so that you don't mute the top two strings. The resultant, slightly dissonant, clash is exactly what you are looking for here. Likewise in the second bar – make sure the F♯ and G notes ring together and savour that sound!

Ex 4

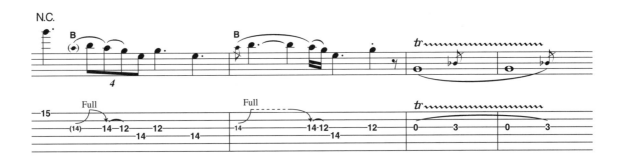

Beck plays a more straightforward blues lick in these bars. Notice that although the harmony is G major he is using an E minor pentatonic shape. This works well as he can play minor bluesy licks but still keep the overall major tonality, as E pentatonic contains all of the notes of a G major chord.

The open string trill is a Beck trademark – use your first finger to hammer-on the B♭ notes.

TECHNIQUEtip

You can use open strings to spice up many different licks, either by using pull-offs, or by incorporating ringing open strings into scale runs. Try working out scales or arpeggios that include open strings and leave them ringing for as long as possible, then savour the effect

EL BECKO

By Tony Hymas and Simon Phillips

© 1980 & 1999 B Feldman & Co Ltd trading as Equator Music Ltd, London WC2H 0EA

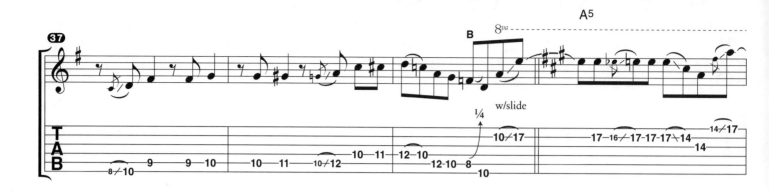

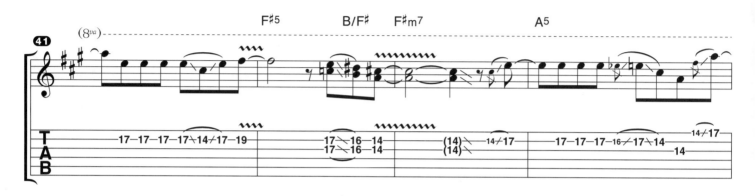

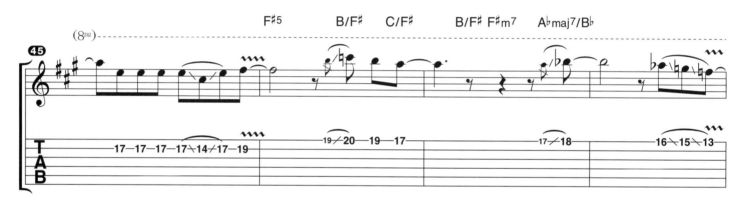

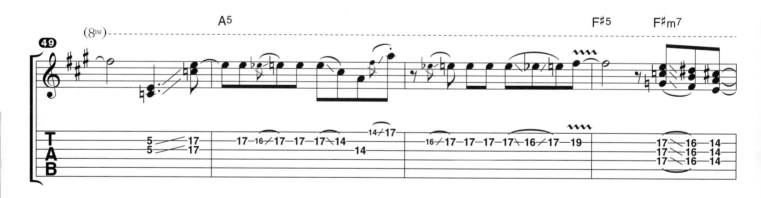

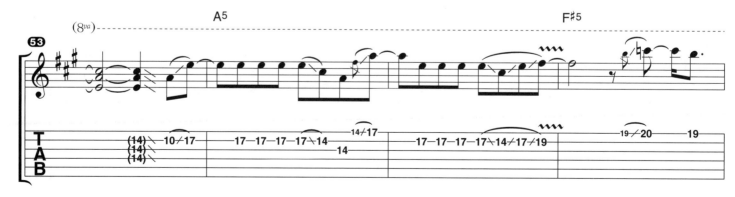

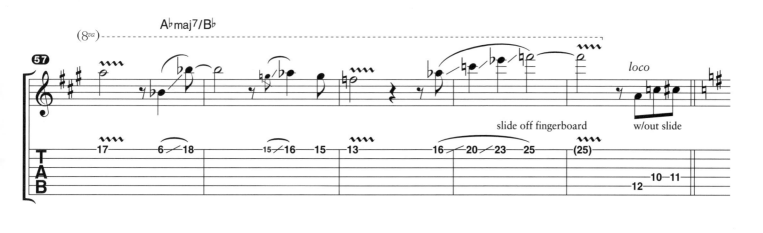

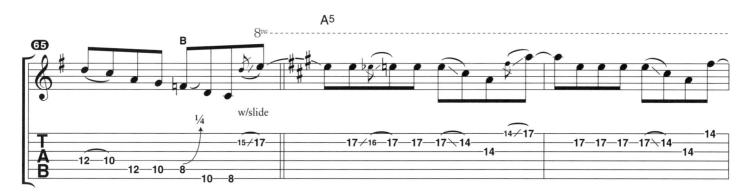

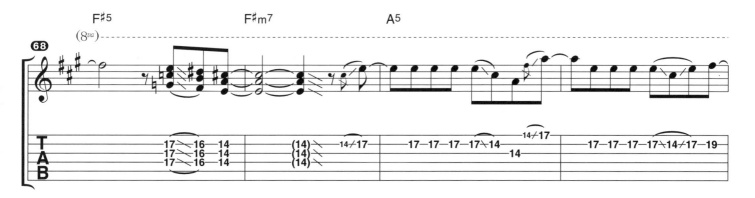

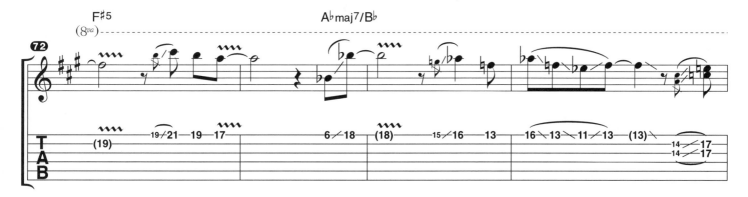

El Becko

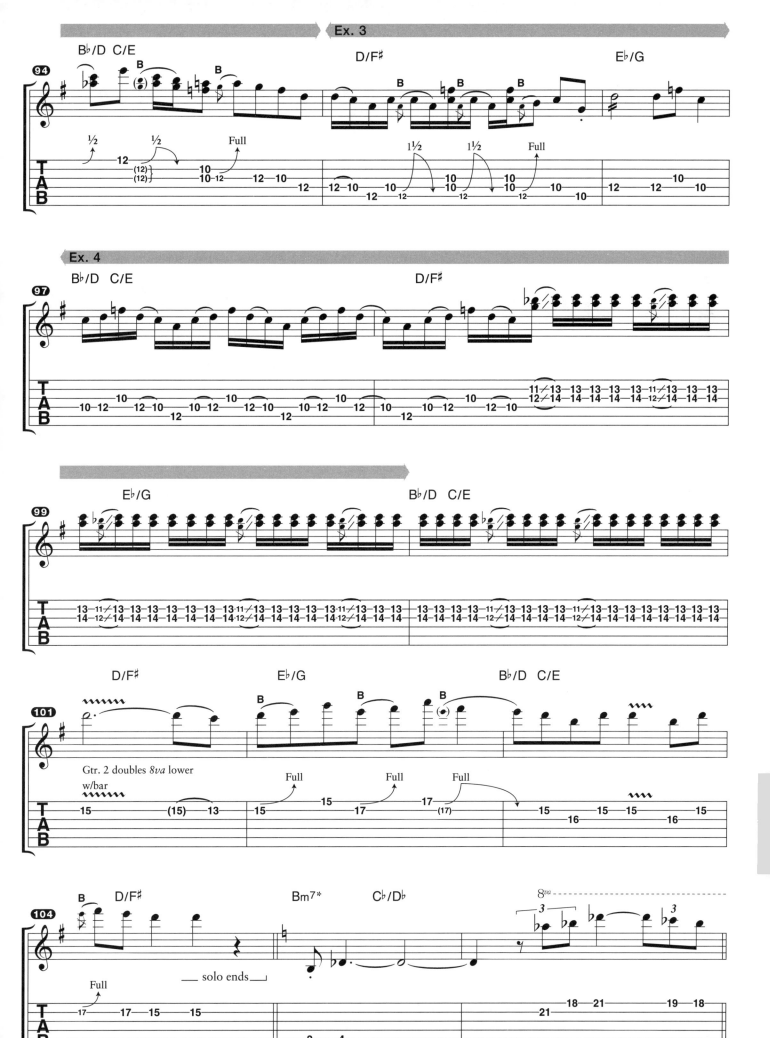

El Becko

The Solo

El Becko

This tune has a great range of feels, from the harmonically rich half-time opening to the no-nonsense rock of the main tune. The solo is played over a half-time chord sequence that gives Beck a stable platform from which to launch his solo. The rest of the tune has a lot of movement, so this section serves to slow the pace a little.

Ex 1

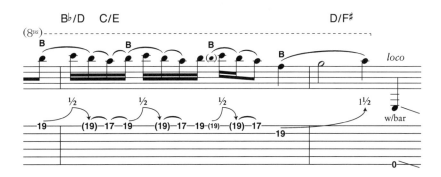

Repeating string bend licks are typical of Beck's style. They are only ½ step bends so you can use either your third or second finger to play them, though you may find the pull-offs to the A note easier if you use your third finger to bend the string.

You will definitely need your third finger for the bend in the second bar – this is a slow bend up from F♯ to A on the B string. Take your time over it and make the most of the tension it creates.

Ex 2

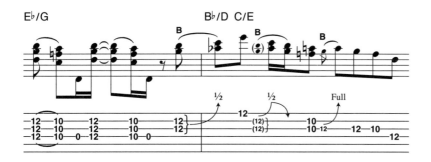

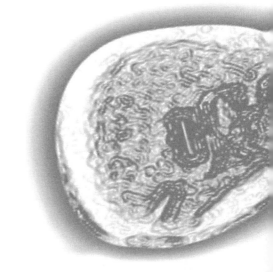

To pull-off these triple stops you'll need to use your first and third fingers to barre the strings. Flatten your third finger over the D, G and B strings at the 12th fret, then pull-off to your first finger, which is holding a barre at the 10th fret.

For the double bend at the end of the first bar, you should use your second and third fingers on the G and B strings respectively, then play the top string with your fifth finger.

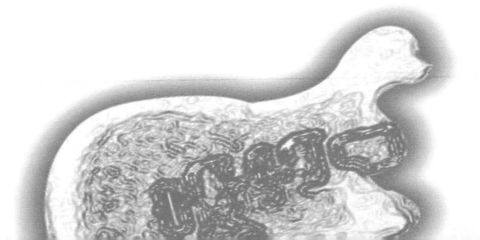

Ex 3

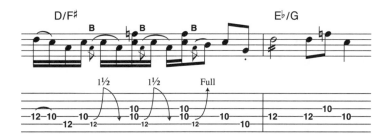

Here is another example of Beck's trademark bending lick. The A string is being bent by 1½ steps, so be sure to use your third finger and support it with two others. As the A string is too close to the edge of the neck to bend it in the normal direction, towards the bottom string, you'll need to bend away from you, towards the floor. This lick ends with a tremolo-picked D note – Beck was probably using a pick for this tune, but he gave them up shortly afterwards.

TECHNIQUEtip

If you are not using a pick and want to simulate the effect of tremolo-picking, do what Jeff does – fake it. Use your first finger supported by your thumb as a temporary pick to play rapidly repeating notes.

Ex 4

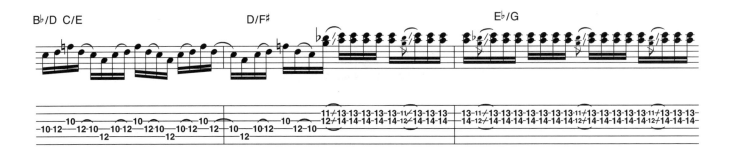

Notice how this simple repeating pattern crosses the beat in an interesting way. This is a good way to add to your soloing vocabulary – take simple melodic ideas and use rhythmic variety to enhance them.

Use alternate picking to play this, starting with a downstroke. This will allow you to work up to speed more easily.

In the second and third bars Jeff plays another simple idea, this time using sliding double-stops. Here again it's the rhythm that makes it interesting. Use your first and second fingers to hold down the G and B strings.

76 *El Becko*